# On the Reef

by Sarah Snashall

OXFORD
UNIVERSITY PRESS

# Meet the Reef

There are lots of animals.

Little animals form the coral.
Look at the coral.

# Food on the Reef

Fun fish fill the reef.
Some get food from the coral.

Some fish feed on plants.

Sharks come to the reef.
They swim near to the fish.

fin
reef shark
gills
tail

# Keep Hidden

Some animals keep hidden.
The reef helps them.

Do you see the eel?
It keeps out of sight.

Some animals have hard shells.
This one likes the weeds.

Can you see a crab peeking out?

Can you see the crab?
The shell looks like coral.

Can you see the fish?
It looks like a rock.

# Reef Visit

Some rubbish sinks down
to the reef.
It can harm the animals.

Avoid putting rubbish in the reef.

goatfish

shark

eel

coral

crab

Encourage students to read the animal names and match them to the pictures.